With love
from

_____

to

_____

LITTLE ☆ STARS™

AQUARIUS

A parent's guide to the little star of the family

JOHN ASTROP

with illustrations by the author

E L E M E N T
Shaftesbury, Dorset ● Rockport, Massachusetts
Brisbane, Queensland

© John Astrop 1994

Published in Great Britain in 1994 by
Element Books Ltd.
Longmead, Shaftesbury, Dorset

Published in the USA in 1994 by
Element, Inc.
42 Broadway, Rockport, MA 01966

Published in Australia in 1994 by
Element Books Ltd.
for Jacaranda Wiley Ltd.
33 Park Road, Milton, Brisbane, 4064

All rights reserved.
No part of this book may be reproduced or utilized
in any form or by any means, electronic or mechanical,
without permission in writing from the Publisher.

Printed and bound in Great Britain by
BPC Paulton Books Ltd.

British Library Cataloguing in Publication
data available

Library of Congress Cataloguing in publication
data available

ISBN 1-85230-547-9

CONTENTS

THE TWELVE SIGNS

Everyone knows a little about the twelve sun signs. It's the easiest way to approach real astrology without going to the trouble of casting up a chart for the exact time of birth. You won't learn everything about a person with the sun sign but you'll know a lot more than if you just use observation and guesswork. The sun is in roughly the same sign and degree of the zodiac at the same time every year. It's a nice astronomical event that doesn't need calculating. So if you're born between

May 22 and June 21 you'll be pretty sure you're a Gemini; between June 22 and July 23 then you're a Cancer and so on. Many people say how can you divide the human race into twelve sections and are there only twelve different types. Well for a start most people make assessments and judgements on their fellow humans with far smaller groups than that. Rich and poor, educated and non-educated, town girl, country boy, etc. Even with these very simple pigeon holes we can combine to make 'Rich educated town boy' and 'poor non-educated country girl'. We try to get as much information as we can about the others that we make relationships with through life. Astrology as a way of describing and understanding others is unsurpassed. Take the traditional meaning of the twelve signs:

Aries - is self-assertive, brave, energetic and pioneering.

Taurus - is careful, possessive, values material things, is able to build and make things grow.

Gemini - is bright-minded, curious, communicative and versatile.

Cancer - is sensitive, family orientated, protective and caring.

Leo - is creative, dramatic, a leader, showy and generous.

Virgo - is organised, critical, perfectionist and practical.

Libra - is balanced, diplomatic, harmonious, sociable, and likes beautiful things.

Scorpio - is strong-willed, magnetic, powerful, extreme, determined and recuperative.

Sagittarius - is adventurous, philosophical, far-thinking, blunt, truth seeking.

Capricorn - is cautious, responsible, patient, persistent and ambitious.

Aquarius - is rebellious, unorthodox, humanitarian, idealistic, a fighter of good causes.

Pisces - is sensitive, imaginative, caring, visionary and sacrificing.

If you can find anyone in your circle of friends and acquaintances who isn't described pretty neatly by one of the above it would be surprising. Put the twelve signs into different lives and occupations and you see how it works. A Taurean priest would be more likely to devote his life to looking after the physical and material needs of his church members, feeding the poor, setting up charities. A Virgoan bank robber would plan meticulously and never commit spontaneous crimes. A Leo teacher would make learning an entertainment and a pleasure for her pupils.

So with parents and children. A Capricorn child handles the business of growing up and learning in a very different way to a Libran child. A Scorpio parent manages the family quite differently to an Aquarian. The old boast, 'I'm very fair, I treat all my children the same', may not be the best way to help your little ones at all. Our individual drive is the key to making a success of life. The time when we need the most acceptance of the way we are is in childhood. As a parent it's good to know the ways in which our little ones are like us but we must never forget the ways in which they are different.

LITTLE AQUARIUS

If your excited mother-in-law asks you whether it's going to be a girl or a boy and should she knit pink or blue booties, tell her it's an Aquarian and vermilion with yellow spots and heels that light up would do nicely. The all-electric family eccentric has arrived and you might as well start as he or she means to go on! Little Aquarians are made for the world of the future and not the past. They come on to this planet with plans, so get ready to clear away all that stuff that has gone before. Four or five millenniums, what did they know! The most original and inventive little characters in the zodiac, small Aquarians are the ultimate Air signs. Their quest is for knowledge and they question everything, turning it up on end and sideways just to see if it works better that way.

These individualists are part of the illustrious group of humanity that change the course of history, not so much by becoming great politicians, poets and generals, but by inventing sliced bread, space travel or the tin-opener. There is a 'go it alone' quality about all Aquarians that enables them to carry on with their obsessions, causes or crazes regardless of the jibes and sneers of dull

old fuddy-duddies like the rest of us. In fact they don't give a hoot what we think. This all sounds  like your new little star isn't going to be very sociable, and won't have many friends. Wrong! Aquarians love all humanity, their fellow man, woman and child. Nearly always, whatever their chosen occupation, they have a second important string to their bow. You can bet that wherever there's a good cause to fight on behalf of the less fortunate, there'll be an Aquarian taking time off work and up front with a banner. They are the most loyal friends, trust 'em, you won't find too many hypocrites amongst Aquarians, they just don't have to bother. What they say, they mean, take it or leave it! They even go out of their way to shock just to stop us all taking our comfortable little grooves too seriously. If the film 'Amadeus' was accurate, the great Mozart couldn't have been more outrageously Aquarian. Jackson Pollock gave us a bit of a shock too! You'll realise now that Lewis Carroll's Wonderland was really just a nice comfortable home from home for an Aquarian. Stangely enough, just to keep up the oddity the Water-Carrier is not a Water sign involved with seeing life filtered through the emotions. Air signs take a much more detached view of the world, the Aquarian symbol representing the enlightened person pouring out wisdom and justice on to the world. You'll remember that when your little Aquarian, at breakfast, asks you where is Ethiopia and what would it cost to send a parcel there?

THE BABY

Little Aquarians often arrive into this world suddenly, unexpected (everyone said he was going to be a Pisces!) or late. Either way, whatever super-system or smooth-running routines you've planned will be redundant the moment this babe arrives. You'll never be quite sure when it's feeding time, nappy changing time, or sleep time. One

 thing is certain: whatever the pattern turned out to be today, it'll be different tomorrow. Timetables usually have to be thrown out of the window in favour of playing everything by ear.

This goes for baby's development too, strange food likes and dislikes start earlier than most. This is the babe that may walk before he can crawl and then, discovering crawling, refuse to

walk anywhere for the next few months. Baby Aquarians have a different kind of stubbornness to the little Taurean; it is just that, whatever you like to try and coax them into, they have to find out things for themselves! Aquarians are great communicators and they're going to do a great deal of fast talking in their lives, so the sooner you start to chat with this little one the better. They learn fast in this area and you'll be surprised how soon you're not talking baby talk. How else is your Aquarian babe going to be able to question every decision you make?

The First Three Years

Life, once the small Aquarian is mobile, will become a series of decisions – which little rebellions to allow and which to stand firm on. Clamping down on all sullen little 'Nos' will just produce more and more. Don't forget questioning is little Aquarius's important drive and has to be practised in order to start formulating personal ideas and understanding the world. Your little Water-Carrier, seeing all people as equal even in these first tender years, will respond to good sensible arguments and logic a lot easier than parental insistence. Potty training, like all the other phases in your small Aquarian's development, may come early or it may come late. What's more than likely is it will finally only be achieved as long as the call of nature is accompanied by a small tune on the toy xylophone resting on his knees and a peanut butter sandwich in his other hand. Gadgets and especially electrical equipment will be an utter fascination to your little inventor. Always on the look out for some new bit of technical information, small Aquarius's probing fingers will have to be watched constantly. The mass of wires at the back of a midi music system is happy hunting ground for this bright spark. Get in there quick with an alternative but make it something complicated and something she's never played with before. In the first few years little Aquarius's conversational talents, having exercised themselves extensively with you, will flow easily into popularity with the world of little friends. Lots of socialising keeps this one busy and the rebellions fewer and further between.

THE KINDERGARTEN

The hurly-burly of boisterous nursery school life will be easy enough for your little 'original' to take in one bounding stride. Lots of new people to be challenged, surprised, entertained and shocked (in the nicest possible way of course): 'not that way, this way, put it upside down, why don't we eat it!' All great fun although most of the toys and games will be all too familiar to your little one and more interesting inventions will be bound to manifest themselves. 'I'm afraid Emily has managed to melt all the school plasticine whilst mendin' the

radiators for us!' Friends will be made and dropped just as quickly in favour of a new arrival in the class. Never close and clinging, but preferring lots of friends, Aquarians often make a buddy out of the loneliest little feller in the nursery school just 'cos it isn't fair. For a day or two anyway.

SCHOOL AND ONWARDS

Aquarians are usually bright as buttons but, of course, in their own special way. Their minds are always working and often in class they will be accused of daydreaming. It takes a lot to hold the attention of a little Aquarian if it's just a matter of feeding in facts. Little Water-Carriers don't daydream. Like absent-minded professors, they can walk into closed doors and trip on their own shadows. Yes, their minds are busy on other things: a new way to programme an alarm watch to time the next litter of kittens Tabitha is expecting, how to

harness the power of the school water fountain and a bicycle pump to propel the latest design of paper rocket. When Aquarians work hard they can show brilliance if not occasionally genius. When they don't they could be on another planet. A social conscience even in the earliest years will get your fair-thinking youngster supporting good causes and working out of school hours on humanitarian projects. School work will always be up and down but only because other things sometimes will occupy that quicksilver mind. Things that will turn up later to surprise you and the rest of us when they make their successful, but original, way in life.

The Three Different
Types of Aquarius

THE DECANATES

Astrology traditionally divides each of the signs into three equal parts of ten degrees called the decanates. These give a slightly different quality to the sign depending on whether the child is born in the first, second or third ten days of the thirty-day period when one is in a sign. Each third is ruled by one of the three signs in the same element. Aquarius is an Air sign and the three Air signs are Aquarius, Gemini and Libra. The nature of Air signs is basically communicative so the following three types each has a different way of expressing the way in which they communicate.

First Decanate - Jan. 21 to Jan. 30

This is the part of Aquarius that is most typical of the sign qualities. Aquarius is a rebel. They take a good look at, and point out to us, things that have been around too long and have outworn their use. They look at injustices that have carried on and on because nobody else noticed and they make us do something about them. They are the catalysts for change in our society and although they sometimes make the traditionalists amongst us feel uncomfortable we would have seized up and come to a standstill in our own little grooves centuries ago without them. They can change our ideas on painting, fashion, music, writing, politics and even humour. Oprah Winfrey even gets us telling all the terrible things we do to each other on prime time TV. How does she do that? The romantic poet Lord Byron, though quite ill at the time, recruited a regiment in the cause of Greek independence against the Turks in 1823 and was made commander-in-chief of their forces the following year.

Second Decanate - Jan. 31 to Feb. 9

This is the Intellectual Rebel and is the part of Aquarius that shares the influence of Mercury and Gemini. OK, they're not all intellectuals, but what they do is largely the result of thought processes and it is in communication rather than actions that they realise their best potential. Your young Aquarian born in this period will be adept at the use of words and quick to invent interesting new ways of doing things. These are less followers of great causes than the previous decanate but rather they are innovators in whatever field they choose to specialise. Dickens wrote popular fiction for people that had never been interested in literature before. His early works were the first to be issued in monthly instalments. Also from this decanate are writers that experimented with words themselves in new and almost eccentric ways like James Joyce and Gertrude Stein. In the rock world, where to be outrageous is the norm, Alice Cooper stands out in the crowd!

Third Decanate - Feb. 10 to Feb. 19

This is the Diplomatic Rebel where the qualities of Aquarius have the added influences of Libra and Venus. This is the most contradictory part of the sign – a strange mixture of the Aquarian desire to shock with the Libran desire to please. It softens the 'cut out the beating around the bush' quality of the more aggressive first decanate but in no way lessens the end results. They just manage things with a rare Aquarian commodity, 'tact'. These Aquarians want peace and harmony as well as change for the better and tread a difficult tightrope in order to get it. Abraham Lincoln's brilliant speeches, timing and open-mindedness won him a place amongst the greatest Presidents America has ever seen. In typical Aquarian eccentricity, albeit harmonious, Yoko Ono joined Libran John Lennon in trying to get world peace from a comfortable bed. Prime Minister Harold Macmillan convinced the British, for a while, that they'd 'Never had it so good!'. Little Thomas Edison, despite what his Mum said, kept on playing with electrical gadgets! Was that the phone ringing, Tom?

OTHER LITTLE AQUARIANS

Mums and Dads like you delighted in bringing up the following little rebels. Yours will probably turn out to be even more famous!

First Decanate Aquarius

Jackson Pollock, Wolfgang Amadeus Mozart, Lewis Carroll, Colette, W. Somerset Maugham, Oprah Winfrey, Paul Newman, John Belushi, Christian Dior, Virginia Woolf, Benny Hill, Lord Byron, Anton Chekhov, Jeanne Moreau, Franklin D. Roosevelt, Vanessa Redgrave, Germaine Greer.

Second Decanate Aquarius

Franz Peter Schubert, Zane Grey, Norman Mailer, James Joyce, Gertrude Stein, Fernand Léger, Charles Lindberg, Charles Dickens, Juliette Greco, Jules Verne, Franz Marc, Lana Turner, Jack Lemmon, James Dean, Philip Glass, Bob Marley, Zsa Zsa Gabor, Norman Wisdom, Alice Cooper, Ronald Reagan, Mia Farrow, Carole King.

Third Decanate Aquarius

Yoko Ono, Len Deighton, Burt Reynolds, Mary Quant, Jimmy Durante, Harold Macmillan, Bertold Brecht, Joyce Grenfell, Thomas Edison, Max Baer, Abraham Lincoln, Charles Darwin, Georges Simenon, Kim Novak, Jack Benny, Alan Bates, Jack Palance, John Travolta, Helen Gurley Brown.

And Now the

Parents

THE ARIES PARENT

The good news!

Nothing complicated about you, you're just enthusiastic, optimistic, energetic and a power-house of support to your loved ones, friends and anyone else that takes your fancy! Aries love a challenge and will be totally involved in keeping up with this future-orientated wonder. Little Aquarians are original, inventive and masters of the unexpected. They approach life in the spirit of the explorer accepting little at face value, questioning everything, turning things upside down, looking

at them from every angle and trying them on for size. No little traditionalists these babes, they've come in to the old-fashioned computer age to tell us what's coming next. The Aries parent's individuality will respond with admiration for the little Water-Carrier's natural self-confidence that refuses to conform to the norm. You are very affectionate and sometimes little Aquarius may seem detached and even absent-minded when it comes to close family affections but you'll get your allocation if you stand in line. It just has to be shared with the dog, the milkman, Star Trek, and an ever-changing bevy of oddball 'friends'. Little Aquarius is as dogged as you when on to a challenging project but it has to be his own and only he knows how to go about it. Wave flags of encouragement, but tie this one down to your Aries objectives and expectations and you'll find the leash strained to the limit. Encourage and support 'doing one's own thing'. It shouldn't be hard as that's what you've done all your life. Work together but each do it your own way. Best activities to share with your small mad inventor are plenty of junk boxes full of screws, nuts, bolts, etc.; mechanical gadgets to convert; simple science books; anything about different people and cultures.

...and now the bad news!

'Actions speak louder than words.' There's only one Aquarian answer to that old Aries motto,

'No they don't!' In this relationship reason, respect and logic are better peacemakers than heavy-handed authority. If you don't want confrontations fourteen times every day, get talking. You want something done, give a reason. You want little Aquarius to stop doing something, give a reason. This is a relationship of equals, you better believe it! Junior thinks you're equal to him any day!

THE TAURUS PARENT

The good news!

You are the ideal easy-going but well-organised parent. The Taurean, the envy of many less efficient parents, can set up perfect routines that make everyone's lives around them run smoothly, comfortably and efficiently. Everyone knows that - except the young Aquarian. Good proven ways hold no water for this miniature revolutionary. From earliest years, small Aquarians think for themselves, mentally experimenting and communicating their controversial ideas to all that may present them with a ready-made rule. Taurean thoroughness (with a great deal of loosening up and staying well in the background) can provide a firm home base for the long-range exploits of this free spirit. Little Aquarians never seem to share the average child's need to conform in order to feel secure. Indifferent to what the others wear, think and do, these young eccentrics maintain their unique individuality whilst still being a most welcome member of the 'gang'. How they do that when all the other kids are desperately trying to be just like everyone else you may never find out.

One thing is certain, you just can't boss around little folk like this. The Taurean will find that plenty of friendly discussion on all subjects achieves far more than heavy 'guidance'. Fortunately a stubborn old Taurean like you won't feel obliged to give in every time, and the Aquarian need to fight for ideas and causes will increase this child's confidence and common sense in these day-to-day encounters. Fifty-fifty sounds fair but you may have to settle for sixty-forty! You take a pride in your home being full of the best comforts around; well, your little humanitarian will want to share it with all and sundry so put on loose covers. The wear and tear that one extremely sociable little Aquarian generates may surprise you.

...and now the bad news!

You can take a lot more than almost any sign in the zodiac before you begin to lose patience, but

even you can be pushed too far. There will undoubtedly be experiments by little Aquarius, made
just to find out just how far that is. Met with your
deadly weapon, stubbornness, the game can go
sour with your small rebel deliberately attempting
to shock you with outbursts of outrageous and
antisocial behaviour. It'll have to be resolved
with discussion and reason will prevail, even if it
is an agreement to respect each other's different
opinions.

♊

THE GEMINI PARENT

The good news!

You've never quite lost the joy of your own childhood with your quicksilver mind and your busy fingers. Always open to new ideas, even bright Gemini may have to open wider for nutty little Aquarius. Unpredictable, amusing, and often unashamedly eccentric, the little Aquarian flouts convention and questions everything. Born inventors, small Water-Carriers insist on discovering for themselves and doing everything their own way. This unusual and independent approach should stimulate and delight the sharp-minded Gemini, providing a fine recipe for a close, friendly, talkative relationship with a good measure of argument. Healthy debate is a must. These youngsters need a good constant to push against in order to establish their own unique ideas and successful self-confidence. Like sociable Gemini, little Aquarians are easy 'mixers', taking quickly to kindergarten and school life with few problems

and no tearful partings. Both of you can be a little detached where the emotional side of life is concerned but if you neglect the hugs of affection, forgetting them in the midst of all your good companionable conversations, your little one may become a little inept at showing feelings. Talking fast over held-in emotions can become a typically Aquarian nervous reaction to being unsure of emotions. Share a few 'weepie' movies every now and again and let yourselves go. Poor little Bambi! Your small fighter of good causes will take on her first challenge. Nasty huntsman!

...and now the bad news!

Clashes between these 'good communications' experts should be few, and probably the only danger is Gemini's open mind allowing too much freedom. Aquarians, with nothing to kick against, will go to extremes of outrageous behaviour, using shock tactics in order to find the limits. No prison bars, but a few strategically placed fences help. Keep the activities shared and varied, with masses of odds and ends, bits and bobs to invent things with, reference books, space-age toys, Dad's first old 8k computer, and keep open house to little friends (they'll be a strange mixture too); don't forget pets to bring out the caring parts.

THE CANCER PARENT

The good news!

Ever heard of a Cancerian that didn't dote on their adorable offspring? No of course not and you're just going to love this little star to bits! The warm, caring, and humour-loving Cancer parent will delight in the antics of this inscrutable little Aquarian eccentric. Bubbling with curiosity, outrageously nonconformist, but far too sociable to be really unruly, this freedom-fighter will bring out the best of Cancer's imaginative abilities. Cancer will respond to, and encourage, young Aquarius's love of group activity, though with perhaps just a twinge of remorse when Junior rushes into play-school on the very first day without even a backward glance. Cancerians are much too clever to lay down a firm set of rules for running the family without disguising them as something else. Parent and child in this inventive and imaginative relationship will easily find ways to make dull and necessary routine a new adventure every day.

Aquarians, no matter how young, can often seem like absent-minded professors with a detachment and aloofness that is almost a challenge to Cancer's need for closeness. Demonstrative as you are, you may have to approach the hugs and

cuddles side of the relationship with a little more reserve than with other more emotionally driven children. Keep it going in little doses and you may have, later on, an emotionally confident large Aquarius. The Cancerian instinct for protectiveness makes for a lot of extra worries with a small Aquarian. You worry anyway, but the constant unexpected actions that the little Water-Carrier surprises you with could make you end up a nervous wreck unless you relax a little. They're self-reliant quite early but, if you're constantly stepping in to help, you set this contrary one in yet another direction and can precipitate the small disaster you were trying to avert. Relax, little Aquarians have eccentric, but capable, guardian angels as well.

...and now the bad news!

The difficulties, if they ever occur, will be concerned with the Cancerian habit of looking back and the Aquarian need to look forward. There can be big disagreements if you expect little Aquarius to always want to repeat the pleasure that you had last time. 'You know you liked it, you had a marvellous time last time we went', falls on deaf ears to this 'Done that, what's next' character. Little Aquarius is not being ungrateful, but holding back the forward-looking advance feels like limitation to this one. Aquarians react explosively to undue restriction of their freedom. This one's a delightful friend but never a treasured possession.

♌

THE LEO PARENT

The good news!

The fact that you and your child are opposite in terms of their zodiac signs can be both a help and a hindrance. Whichever it does it will certainly keep the relationship stimulating and great fun. You Leos make generous, loving parents who will do everything in their power to give their children the best things in life, and as such expect a certain amount of recognition, if not adulation, from their offspring. Aquarius Junior, a human rights supporter from the cradle, is reluctant to bow down to anyone, and that includes Leo Ma and Pa! Water-Carriers give great respect though – where it's due – and to just about anyone that they consider deserves it. Thus friends and acquaintances (which will be staggeringly large in number) will comprise every conceivable variety of the species. The Leo parent, host par excellence, will be given ample opportunity to keep open house for this

motley entourage. The motley part may sometimes seem to be a little extreme to the proud Lion, taken aback with this little Aquarian's love of the under-dog. Effusive and demonstrative, Leo loves the physical contact of bear hugs, piggy backs, tick-ling etc., and may find it hard to accept little Aquarius's detachment and independence. The name of the game is to treat this youngster as an equal. From an early age, discussion of the world at large will produce quick understanding and unique Aquarian views.

...and now the bad news!

Always falling into the leading position when arguments occur, Leo must realise that the auto-cratic approach is out; any attempt to take over and lay down the law without explaining the whys and wherefores to the intellectually orientated little one will only arouse the rebel at the heart of every

Aquarian and spoil what could be a beautiful friendship. This doesn't mean giving in every time for, just to be contrary, your little one needs a little resistance to pit the Aquarian strength against. Keeping the balance can be a good exercise for both of you. Better still are plenty of shared challenges. You think big and getting little Aquarius to help plan projects will be an entertainment and always a surprise with this little inventor.

THE VIRGO PARENT

The good news!

Virgos can be the best, most responsible and reliable parents in the book! You like order, system and efficiency, set up good routines and stick to them. That's just what little children want to make them feel secure and loved. Sorry, not all of 'em, at least it often won't seem so with your small rebel! Little Aquarians thrive on the unexpected, the unpredictable, the untried and the new. This may make the two of you seem an incompatible duo but in fact it can work very well for both.

Though Junior needs to kick against rules and regulations, Virgo's well-reasoned ones will more than stand the test, which was all that little Aquarius wanted to find out anyway. These small rebels question everything, accepting nothing at face value. In this way they develop their own individual approach and early self-confidence. Virgo's good down-to-earth answers to this little one's probing arguments should provide a healthy dialogue and stimulating relationship. Providing a good balance between reasonable guidelines and a fair share of freedom may be a touch like

walking a tightrope but the rewards are great. These little Water-Carriers are amongst us to knock down the fuddy-duddy outmoded ideas, replacing them with more workable ones to take us into the future. Your greatest delight, being quite bright-minded yourself, will be in little Aquarius's inventiveness. Typically loony but workable answers to ordinary everyday problems will keep you in hysterics. Finding the dinner plates outside in the rain for an easy washing-up session may seem like Junior being lazy, but it's always funny! As soon as little Aquarius discovers the world outside family life, the friends start to roll in. Face the fact, the parent of a small Aquarian that keeps open house keeps a happy Aquarian.

...and now the bad news!

Being a bit of an old perfectionist, there will be times when the picky side of Virgo just has to take you over! You should have learnt in the first few years that nothing your little one does is going to be 'right'. It might be an interesting alternative way of doing things, but it won't be 'Virgo right'. In response to the inevitable nagging, all the Aquarian invention will be thrown into avoidance of doing anything, anywhere about the house. Some even show genius in this direction. Remember the old Water-Carrier's motto: 'If a thing's worth doing, it's worth doing the other way.'

THE LIBRA PARENT

The good news!

Both of you are Air signs and both are great thinkers. With good, but not like, minds you'll share a love of sociability and excellent company that should make you the best of pals. The differences in your thinking will keep the conversations alive and full of interest. Libra always sees both sides of a question, balancing each against the other in order to come to a fair decision. Little Aquarius sees all four sides of a question, turns it over, tries it upside down, shakes it, and decides that it was the wrong question anyway. Junior's thought processes are the stuff of inventors, geniuses and eccentrics. No one could enjoy this always lively companion more than you. The Libran's need for close relationships makes for sensitivity to the wishes of others, and they'll bend over backwards to please and keep their children happy. Little Aquarians have no desire to live up to anybody's expectations; take them or leave them they don't mind. These nonconformists set up their own way of life from the earliest years, seeming to have none of the usual child's insecurity about looking or acting different from the rest. Their role in life is to explore the ultimate in possibilities, and rules and regulations are

never going to be accepted without question. This never seems to make them misfits though, and you'll see from the succession of little visitors how high on the popularity stakes your youngster really is. Little Aquarius needs more than just chat to keep happy, for the real Aquarian invention needs gadgets and stuff! You will be well rewarded if you provide the biggest box of old gadgets, clocks, typewriters, torches, beads, nuts and bolts, you can find. The infinite pleasure to little Aquarius will only be surpassed by her first computer.

...and now the bad news!

Easy-going Libra sets up few rules, hopefully providing a good diplomatic balance as and when each situation occurs. However, Junior will need a few brick walls to scale and the 'anything for a quiet life' Libran attitude can leave this little one a rebel without a cause. Unfortunately, without some lines drawn little Aquarius will always be impelled to behave as outrageously and obstinately contrarily as possible. Not quite so much a cry for help as a pain in the neck. Come on Libra, balance the giving in with a little firm resistance and plenty of good humour and little Aquarius will settle for a daily refreshing argument that will keep both of you happy.

THE SCORPIO PARENT

The good news!

You Scorpios rarely let the talents of your children gather dust. Quick to sense their strengths and weaknesses, you will be a constant support if not a driving force in your offspring's early years. That is, with any ordinary child. The Aquarian child, however, is a very different kettle of fish. Inventive, impulsive, unusual, original and almost impossible to pin down. The heavy, dogmatic side of Scorpio will find an argumentative rebel, the ever-loving hug may get an indifferent shrug, and attempts to get some order into Junior's life will be met with an absent-minded attitude. Once the sheer surprise is overcome and fresh angles have been sorted out, Scorpio can put in some good work towards developing the individualist that is already there. Little Aquarius questions everything and Scorpio probably has all the answers to keep this relationship happily sizzling. It may be difficult at first for powerful, loving Scorpio to understand that little Aquarius works better on a friendship level. Not overly affectionate, young Aquarians share their unlimited friendship equally with all and sundry – friends, parents, other kids'

parents, dogs, cats – you name it, they befriend it. There's no room for Scorpio possessiveness with this social mixer; this one's looking to you as a friend, not as a boss. Your strong protective instinct may make you want to step in whenever your little one looks like getting into trouble. Resist, for this is not the way an original thinker learns to develop self-reliance. Never intimidated by adults, little Aquarians judge them just as they would one of their school buddies, all equal. The little Water-Carrier hates rules, but taking them away is not the answer and could leave a lot of energy with nowhere to go. That spells trouble. Keep the rules but keep them fair.

...and now the bad news!

The old Scorpio trick of holding in feelings until ready to burst results in the occasional emotional explosion (dare I say, well out of proportion to whatever lit the fuse – yes I dare, I'm a Scorpio too). When this happens as a result of one of little Aquarius's more exasperating eccentricities it can become an exciting new shocking example to your little one that will be elaborated on ad infinitum. If you can do it so can I. Don't forget we're all equal in the eyes of Aquarius. Nuff said!

THE SAGITTARIUS PARENT

The good news!

Sagittarian Fire and Aquarian Air, great for hot-air balloons. Up, up and away! This is a meeting of the zodiac's two freedom-lovers. Sagittarians warm, adventurous, energetic, always looking for new paths to tread, and Aquarians questioning every rule and regulation in the book in order to establish their own individual and uniquely original ideas. Different manifestations of basically the same idea – the search for knowledge and truth. The tolerant Sagittarian will put few limitations on

Junior's actions, however unusual or nonconformist they are, but will give the right kind of straight-talking information that little Aquarius respects. Sagittarian parents give straight answers to all questions, just what little Aquarius wants. This parent's logic, good sense, and open-mindedness will give little cause for young Aquarius to go to anarchistic extremes in the home. However, Junior's drive to knock against something will be hard to conquer and may have to find outside less desirable windmills to tilt against if you don't put up a little firm resistance occasionally. All this Aquarian drive to rebel can be constructively channelled into shared work for

good causes; little Aquarians flourish with a sympathetic, well-intentioned, battle to enjoy. Both of you need to be fairly detached and free-ranging and once little Aquarius is not quite so little it will be surprising if the busy two of you will get to meet more than once or twice a week. This would be a shame as the potential for long debates and arguments (something you both enjoy immensely) between you two storehouses of philosophy and wisdom is infinite. Maybe it's the view from the hot-air balloon, but your two signs always see the world from a different viewpoint to the rest of us, something that can be shared for a lifetime.

...and now the bad news!

Saying what you mean at all times, regardless of when and where, makes you loved for your honesty, once the rest of us have healed the bruises to our vanity. Hot air is bound to cause a little trouble sometimes. The clashes, if any, will be short-lived as you two rarely hold grudges, but knife-edged Sagittarian 'home truths' will be well met with Aquarian shock tactics in short sharp encounters. The occasional sharp scuffle may well be all that you have to deal with. You make better friends than enemies. So share plenty of visiting and visitors, plenty of outdoor romps and at home provide plenty of broken gadgets from which to make new super-inventions.

THE CAPRICORN PARENT

The good news!

Like most signs that rest side by side in the zodiac circle, yours are very different. It could be said that Capricorn's strongest forte is 'discipline' whilst that of the Aquarian child is 'freedom'. They are not incompatible but at times they will look darned like it! The freedom thing doesn't mean that all young Aquarians are anarchists, but accepting rules and regulations (something that Capricornians conscientiously do), without question just doesn't figure in their way of doing things.

Aquarius is the nonconformist of the zodiac, and children born under this sign feel a strong urge to revolt against existing structures and bring in new ideas. However, give them a good logical reason for doing something and it will find easy acceptance. It's often difficult for a parent to come to terms with a child on a totally different wavelength but if Capricorn can tune in to young Aquarius the possibilities are unlimited. Aquarian children often have inventive, original, scientific minds and will be responsive to encouragement and assistance from Capricorn Senior – the supreme realist – in putting their novel ideas into practice. Though little Aquarians need to

knock against authority it is the balance between reasonable rules and reasonable freedom that will keep this relationship challenging, friendly and productive. If your small Aquarius can gently be taught that a little of your infinite patience might be a great asset to his or her future you will have made a great step. You'll do this better by practical example, working on inventive but demanding projects together. Don't forget though, in your practicality, that little Aquarius is always more concerned with the vision rather than the tiny details necessary to get the project finished. I did say a 'little' of your infinite patience.

...and now the bad news!

Your conscientiousness in running your day to day life and application to your duties, added to little Aquarius's natural independence and sometimes sheer awkwardness, can combine to make your relationship a little out of touch in an emotional sense. Neither of you being naturally demonstrative doesn't mean that each of you can do without it. You get too busy and the little inventor just absent-mindedly forgets. It's a shame for you both so one of you will have to make the first move. It's strange that though Aquarians rarely care what others think, they are often reluctant to make the first move where feelings are concerned.

THE AQUARIUS PARENT

The good news!

When parent and child are born under the same sun sign they usually enjoy a natural empathy, and questions of conflict do not normally arise. It can, however, produce extremes of their particular qualities without a little deliberate and subtle counterbalancing. As Aquarians are, anyhow, nonconformists often taking things to the limits, balance may present a problem and subtlety may be even more impossible. Mutual independence, freedom and tolerance will be demanded and granted in this relationship. Aquarian parents will let their children have their head from an early age and in return will expect to lead a life of their own, free of the excessive demands of an overdependent child. That's fine, but though Junior will knock against authority it's nevertheless important for this little one to have some firm structure or guidelines to avoid becoming a rebel without a cause. Through healthy challenge and argument the little Aquarian forms his or her own unique ideas and

sense of justice. Setting up a strict but reasonable routine, though out of character for the Aquarian parent, will develop Junior's independence and self-confidence more effectively. If you chop and change the routine, which of course you will, as long as the new rules are made clear to your junior partner they will be accepted joyfully as often as they occur. Probably a good Aquarian solution to this problem anyway. Aquarian parents usually realise that being up to the minute with the latest crazes is imperative to all children. This is doubly important with a little Aquarian, so if you're still analog, you better try getting digital!

...and now the bad news!

This is really a problem as I'm not sure that two Aquarians could ever clash in the usual sense because that's what they do anyway. Whatever battles you both choose to have with each other they'll probably never coincide and the other one won't realise that it's going on anyway. Non-battles like this can go on for weeks; as only they could possibly know what they are about, I give up, I'm going to have to draw a slightly bigger illustration below!

THE PISCES PARENT

The good news!

Whereas devoted Piscean parents would go to any lengths to keep their children happy (even overdoing it occasionally with a spot of smother love), Aquarian children just don't like being wrapped in a cosy cocoon and feel the urge to make their own way in the world from a surprisingly early age. Little Aquarians do not need the same amount of protection as the more vulnerable sun signs, and if not granted freedom will demand it as their right. The Piscean's natural anxiety may have to be somewhat compromised. These free-ranging youngsters respond better to logic and reasoning than to pleading; present them with a reasonable argument in favour of something and they'll usually comply. However, do expect little Aquarius to be sometimes outrageously noncon-formist, for in this way these little innovators develop their talent for bringing in the new. Al-though cooler in their affections than emotional Pisces could ever be, they delight in the company of as many friends and playmates as possible. The

way to keep these children happy is to throw open the doors to all and sundry. Little Aquarians are totally unprejudiced and get on with grown-ups as easily as with children. Pisces's delightful sense of fantasy will forge close links with this little one's love of the bizarre and expand the imaginative faculties. Loony imaginative games and crazy conversations will become a popular part of the relationship and encourage Junior's inventive abilities. Both of you work on a mental level and both in your different ways are idealists, so the sharing of bright original ideas and techniques to fight the good causes that you will undoubtedly support, brings you close together.

...and now the bad news!

There should be few clashes for this relationship, but don't forget that your supersensitive awareness of other people's needs and thoughts gets you stepping in just a little too soon, changing anything that may prove tricky for your little one. This won't give Junior the necessary few things to knock against – rebels without a cause get very insecure. Hard to get used to but sometimes leaving them to it when things get difficult or mildly risky achieves more than you could ever hope. Enjoy your little oddball but make sure you allow him to be it!

ON THE CUSP

Many people whose children are born on the day the sun changes signs are not sure whether they come under one sign or another. Some say one is supposed to be a little bit of each but this is rarely true. Adjoining signs are very different to each other so checking up can make everything clear. The opposite table gives the exact Greenwich Mean Time (GMT) when the sun moves into Aquarius and when it leaves. Subtract or add the hours indicated below for your nearest big city.

AMSTERDAM	GMT + 01.00	MADRID	GMT + 01.00
ATHENS	GMT + 02.00	MELBOURNE	GMT + 10.00
BOMBAY	GMT + 05.30	MONTREAL	GMT - 05.00
CAIRO	GMT + 02.00	NEW YORK	GMT - 05.00
CALGARY	GMT - 07.00	PARIS	GMT + 01.00
CHICAGO	GMT - 06.00	ROME	GMT + 01.00
DURBAN	GMT + 02.00	S.FRANCISCO	GMT - 08.00
GIBRALTAR	GMT + 01.00	SYDNEY	GMT + 10.00
HOUSTON	GMT - 06.00	TOKYO	GMT + 09.00
LONDON	GMT 00.00	WELLINGTON	GMT + 12.00

DATE	ENTERS AQUARIUS	GMT	LEAVES AQUARIUS	GMT
1984	JAN 20	9.05 PM	FEB 19	11.16 AM
1985	JAN 20	2.58 AM	FEB 18	5.08 PM
1986	JAN 20	8.47 AM	FEB 18	10.58 PM
1987	JAN 20	2.41 PM	FEB 19	4.50 AM
1988	JAN 20	8.25 PM	FEB 19	10.35 AM
1989	JAN 20	2.07 AM	FEB 18	4.21 PM
1990	JAN 20	8.02 AM	FEB 18	10.14 PM
1991	JAN 20	1.47 PM	FEB 19	3.59 AM
1992	JAN 20	7.33 PM	FEB 19	9.44 AM
1993	JAN 20	1.23 AM	FEB 18	3.35 PM
1994	JAN 20	7.08 AM	FEB 18	9.22 PM
1995	JAN 20	1.01 PM	FEB 19	3.11 AM
1996	JAN 20	6.53 PM	FEB 19	9.01 AM
1997	JAN 20	12.43 AM	FEB 18	2.52 PM
1998	JAN 20	6.46 AM	FEB 18	8.55 PM
1999	JAN 20	12.38 PM	FEB 19	2.47 AM
2000	JAN 20	6.23 PM	FEB 19	8.34 AM
2001	JAN 20	12.17 AM	FEB 18	2.28 PM
2002	JAN 20	6.03 AM	FEB 18	8.14 PM
2003	JAN 20	11.53 AM	FEB 19	2.01 AM
2004	JAN 20	5.43 PM	FEB 19	7.51 PM

John Astrop is an astrologer and author, has written and illustrated over two hundred books for children, is a little Scorpio married to a little Cancerian artist, has one little Capricorn psychologist, one little Pisces songwriter, one little Virgo traveller and a little Aries rock guitarist. The cats are little Sagittarians.